AI Mobility & Balance Systems

How Artificial Intelligence Prevents Falls, Instability, and Loss of Physical Confidence

By Joe Correa

Published by Live Stronger Faster

This book is for educational and informational purposes only. The author and publisher are not engaged in rendering legal, financial, or other professional advice. Readers should consult a qualified professional before making any financial decisions.

First Edition

Table of Contents

Introduction

Mobility is freedom. Balance is confidence. Together, they determine whether aging feels expansive or restrictive. Yet for most people, mobility loss does not arrive suddenly—it begins quietly, years before it is noticed, through subtle changes in gait, reaction time, joint coordination, muscle activation, and neurological feedback loops that slowly reshape how the body moves through space. A slightly shorter stride, a momentary wobble on stairs, hesitation stepping off a curb, or growing avoidance of uneven ground are not "normal aging" milestones; they are early signals of declining balance systems that, left unaddressed, can lead to falls, fear of movement, chronic pain, and loss of independence. This book exists to interrupt that trajectory before it becomes irreversible, using artificial intelligence as a precision tool to protect, restore, and enhance human movement across midlife and beyond.

For decades, fall prevention and balance training were treated as reactive measures—something introduced only after an injury, diagnosis, or visible decline. Medical systems traditionally focused on treating fractures, surgeries, or neurological events rather than preserving the systems that prevent those outcomes in the first place. Artificial intelligence changes this equation entirely. AI allows us to detect instability long before a fall occurs, identify movement asymmetries invisible to the naked eye, and personalize mobility strategies based on how each individual body ages rather than relying on one-size-fits-all recommendations. AI mobility systems do not wait for failure; they work continuously in the background, monitoring movement quality, neuromuscular coordination, and environmental interactions to protect physical confidence at every stage of life.

As we age, balance becomes a whole-body conversation between the brain, nervous system, muscles, joints, vision, inner ear, and even cardiovascular function. Aging disrupts this conversation gradually. Reaction times slow by milliseconds that compound over time. Proprioception—the body's ability to sense its position in space—dulls subtly. Muscle firing sequences become less coordinated. Joint stiffness alters movement mechanics. These changes are often dismissed as "just getting older," yet research consistently shows they are measurable, predictable, and modifiable. Artificial intelligence excels at precisely this kind of pattern recognition. By analyzing thousands of micro-variables simultaneously, AI can detect instability long before it manifests as a stumble, a fall, or fear-based movement avoidance.

This book introduces a new paradigm: proactive mobility intelligence. Instead of waiting for balance to fail, AI-powered systems assess how you walk, stand, turn, rise, and stabilize in real-world conditions. Using data from wearable sensors, smart devices, motion capture, and machine-learning models trained on millions of movement patterns, AI can identify early imbalance signatures unique to your physiology. These insights allow for targeted interventions—specific strength activation, coordination training, neurological stimulation, and environmental adjustments—that preserve mobility while confidence is still intact. The goal is not merely fall prevention, but lifelong movement assurance.

Fear of falling is one of the most underestimated accelerants of physical decline. Once confidence in movement erodes, people unconsciously restrict activity, leading to rapid deconditioning, muscle loss, joint stiffness, and further instability—a vicious cycle that compounds with each passing year. AI mobility systems disrupt this cycle by restoring trust between the mind and body. When individuals receive objective feedback showing improved stability, balance symmetry, and reaction performance, fear diminishes. Movement becomes exploratory again rather than cautious. This psychological dimension of mobility preservation is as critical as the physical one, and AI uniquely bridges both by providing continuous reassurance through data-driven feedback. Another powerful advantage of artificial intelligence is personalization at scale. Traditional balance programs rely on generic exercises that may or may not address the root cause of instability. AI identifies whether imbalance originates from neurological latency, muscular weakness, joint degeneration, vestibular changes, visual dependency, cardiovascular insufficiency, or a combination of factors. This allows interventions to be precisely targeted rather than broadly prescribed. For example, instability driven by delayed muscle firing requires a fundamentally different strategy than instability driven by sensory processing delays or joint degradation. AI distinguishes these pathways with accuracy that was previously unattainable outside specialized clinical labs.

Importantly, AI mobility systems evolve as you do. Aging is not static; it is dynamic. What challenges balance at age 45 differs from what challenges it at 60 or 75. AI systems continuously recalibrate recommendations as your strength, coordination, and neurological responsiveness change over time. This adaptability ensures that mobility support remains relevant rather than outdated, preventive rather than reactive. Instead of periodic checkups that capture a single moment in time, AI provides a living map of your movement health, updating insights in real time.

This book is designed for adults who want to remain physically confident—not just functional—as they age. It is for those who value independence, travel, activity, and autonomy, and who understand that mobility is not about extreme athleticism but about effortless movement through daily life. Whether it is walking confidently on uneven ground, carrying groceries without hesitation, rising from the floor, navigating stairs, or maintaining balance in crowded environments, these everyday movements define quality of life far more than isolated fitness metrics. Artificial intelligence allows us to protect these capabilities intelligently, precisely, and proactively.

Throughout this book, you will learn how AI mobility and balance systems work, what types of data they analyze, how they identify early instability signals, and how they translate insights into actionable strategies. You will explore how AI integrates with wearable technology, home environments, rehabilitation science, and preventive health frameworks to form a comprehensive mobility protection system. The focus is not on replacing human intuition or professional care, but on augmenting it—giving individuals and clinicians deeper insight into movement health before decline becomes visible.

The promise of AI-powered mobility preservation is profound: fewer falls, reduced injury risk, sustained independence, and restored confidence in physical movement across the lifespan.

More importantly, it reframes aging from a process of inevitable loss to one of informed adaptation. By understanding how your balance systems change—and intervening early with intelligent tools—you gain agency over your physical future. This book offers that agency, translating complex AI capabilities into clear, practical understanding that empowers you to move forward with confidence, stability, and freedom at any age.

In the chapters that follow, we will break down the science of balance, the technology behind AI movement analysis, and the practical strategies that transform data into daily resilience. This is not about fearing falls—it is about designing a life where falls become increasingly unlikely because mobility is actively protected. Artificial intelligence is not the future of movement health; it is the present. And for those who choose to use it wisely, it may be one of the most powerful tools ever developed to preserve independence, dignity, and physical confidence throughout aging.

Chapter 1

Understanding the Aging Balance System and Why It Fails

Human balance is not a single function but a complex, constantly adapting system that integrates neurological signaling, muscular coordination, joint mechanics, sensory input, and environmental awareness in real time. Every step taken, every turn made, and every moment spent standing upright depends on the seamless collaboration of these systems operating beneath conscious awareness. In youth, this coordination feels automatic and resilient, capable of absorbing missteps, uneven surfaces, and sudden changes without thought. With age, however, the balance system does not fail abruptly. It degrades incrementally, quietly, and often invisibly, long before any fall occurs. Understanding how and why this happens is the first step toward preventing mobility loss, and artificial intelligence provides unprecedented insight into this process.

At the core of balance lies the nervous system's ability to interpret sensory information and issue corrective commands faster than conscious thought. The brain continuously processes data from the eyes, inner ear, joints, muscles, and skin to determine body position in space. These signals are compared against expected movement patterns learned over decades. When discrepancies arise—such as a slip, tilt, or sudden shift—micro-adjustments are deployed in milliseconds to stabilize posture. Aging subtly alters this feedback loop. Neural transmission slows slightly, sensory acuity dulls, and motor responses lose precision. Individually, these changes seem insignificant, but collectively they increase instability in ways that traditional clinical exams often miss.

Muscle coordination plays an equally critical role. Balance is not about strength alone but about timing, sequencing, and proportional activation. Small stabilizing muscles in the feet, hips, and core must fire at exactly the right moment to maintain equilibrium. Aging disrupts these firing patterns, often due to decreased neuromuscular efficiency rather than muscle loss itself. This leads to delayed responses, compensatory movements, and inefficient stabilization strategies. Over time, the body adapts by becoming more rigid, reducing movement variability to feel safer. Unfortunately, this rigidity increases fall risk rather than reducing it.

Joint health and connective tissue integrity further influence balance. As joints lose range of motion and proprioceptive sensitivity, the brain receives less accurate information about limb position. This creates uncertainty in movement planning, particularly during transitions such as standing up, stepping down, or turning. Vision and vestibular function attempt to compensate, but this compensation becomes increasingly fragile in low-light conditions or on uneven terrain. What appears externally as clumsiness or hesitation is internally a system struggling to reconcile conflicting data streams.

Artificial intelligence excels at identifying these early dysfunctions because it does not rely on subjective observation alone. AI systems analyze thousands of micro-variables simultaneously, including stride variability, weight distribution, joint angles, reaction timing, postural sway, and movement symmetry. Patterns emerge that indicate instability long before it becomes apparent to the individual or clinician. AI does not ask whether balance has failed; it asks how balance is changing, where inefficiencies are emerging, and which subsystems are compensating under stress.

One of the most transformative aspects of AI-driven mobility analysis is its ability to detect asymmetry. Humans naturally favor one side of the body, but aging amplifies these biases. A slight reduction in strength or coordination on one side forces the opposite side to overcompensate, creating a cascade of inefficiencies that increase fall risk. AI systems identify these imbalances quantitatively, allowing for targeted interventions that restore symmetry rather than masking dysfunction with generalized exercises. Environmental interaction is another overlooked factor in balance decline. Flooring type, footwear, lighting, furniture layout, and habitual movement paths all influence stability. AI systems integrate contextual data to assess how individuals move within their actual environments rather than idealized clinical settings. This real-world perspective enables personalized recommendations that improve safety without restricting lifestyle. Instead of advising avoidance, AI enables adaptation.

Perhaps most importantly, AI reframes balance from a static trait to a dynamic process. Balance is not something one either has or loses; it fluctuates daily based on fatigue, stress, hydration, medication, and emotional state. AI systems continuously monitor these fluctuations, providing early warnings when instability thresholds are approached. This allows for timely adjustments—rest, targeted activation, or environmental modification—before a fall becomes likely.

By understanding balance as a system rather than a symptom, individuals gain agency over their mobility trajectory. Artificial intelligence does not replace human awareness; it enhances it, revealing patterns too subtle for intuition alone. This chapter establishes the foundation for proactive mobility preservation, demonstrating that balance decline is neither mysterious nor inevitable. It is measurable, understandable, and—most importantly—modifiable when addressed early with intelligent tools.

"The Day the Floor Felt Different"

Margaret first noticed something was wrong on an ordinary Tuesday morning. Nothing dramatic happened. She didn't fall. She didn't trip. The floor simply felt... different. As she stepped out of bed and walked toward the kitchen, there was a moment—brief but unsettling—where her body hesitated, as if it needed an extra beat to decide where her weight belonged. She brushed it off, telling herself she must have stood up too quickly. At sixty-two, she reasoned, small quirks were to be expected.

Over the following weeks, the moments multiplied. Stepping off curbs required more attention. Turning quickly felt awkward. She began holding railings without realizing it. None of these changes were severe enough to mention to her doctor, and when friends joked about "senior moments," she laughed along, unwilling to see herself reflected in the stereotype. Yet something inside her had shifted. Movement, once effortless, now demanded vigilance.

Margaret was not inactive. She walked daily, did light strength training, and prided herself on staying fit. That made the unease more confusing. When her daughter suggested a wearable mobility assessment device recommended through a wellness program, Margaret agreed reluctantly, convinced it would confirm she was fine. Instead, the data told a different story. The AI analysis revealed subtle delays in her right-side stabilization, increased sway during turns, and a growing reliance on visual cues for balance. None of it was visible to the naked eye. All of it mattered.

What surprised Margaret most was how precise the feedback felt. The system didn't label her as unstable or at risk. It showed trends. It explained how small timing delays in muscle activation were forcing compensations elsewhere. It revealed how fatigue late in the day increased her sway threshold. For the first time, her discomfort had language, structure, and explanation. It wasn't aging—it was adaptation under strain.

With guidance from the AI system, Margaret began targeted interventions. Not generic balance exercises, but specific neuromuscular activations timed to retrain coordination. Environmental adjustments improved lighting and foot placement cues in her home. Movement confidence returned gradually, almost imperceptibly, until one day she realized she had stopped thinking about balance altogether. The floor no longer felt different. It felt trustworthy again.

Months later, Margaret attended a family gathering where an older relative fell while navigating an unfamiliar staircase. As others rushed to help, Margaret felt a quiet gratitude—not relief that it wasn't her, but awareness that it once could have been. She understood now that balance loss doesn't announce itself. It whispers. And with the right tools, those whispers can be heard and answered before they become consequences.

Margaret still aged. Her body still changed. But she moved through the world with restored confidence, knowing that her balance system was no longer a mystery unfolding unchecked. It was a living process she understood, monitored, and supported. Artificial intelligence hadn't made her younger. It had made her aware—and that awareness preserved her freedom.

Chapter 2

How Artificial Intelligence Detects Instability Before Falls Occur

Falls are rarely accidents. They are outcomes. Long before a fall happens, the body broadcasts signals of instability through subtle changes in movement, posture, reaction timing, and coordination. These signals are often imperceptible to the individual experiencing them and frequently missed by traditional assessments that rely on episodic observation rather than continuous analysis. Artificial intelligence fundamentally changes how instability is detected by shifting the focus from isolated events to evolving patterns. Instead of asking whether someone is at risk today, AI evaluates how risk is changing over time, allowing intervention long before balance failure becomes visible or dangerous.

The earliest signs of instability often appear as variability rather than weakness. Small inconsistencies in stride length, foot placement, or weight transfer reveal that the body is compensating for internal inefficiencies. The nervous system begins to hedge its bets, subtly altering movement strategies to preserve safety. These compensations feel adaptive at first, but they create inefficiencies that compound. AI systems are uniquely equipped to detect these micro-variations because they process movement data at a resolution far beyond human perception. By analyzing thousands of data points per second, AI can identify patterns that signal declining balance resilience even when overall performance still appears normal.

One of the most powerful tools AI uses is temporal analysis. Balance is fundamentally about timing. Muscles must activate in precise sequences, sensory signals must arrive without delay, and corrective responses must occur within narrow time windows. Aging disrupts these timelines subtly. A stabilizing muscle fires milliseconds late. A sensory signal arrives slightly delayed. A corrective step is fractionally slower. Individually, these changes are inconsequential. Collectively, they increase the likelihood that the body cannot recover from an unexpected perturbation. AI models trained on large datasets of human movement can detect these timing shifts early, mapping them against known trajectories of instability.

Postural sway analysis is another critical dimension. Even when standing still, the body is constantly making micro-adjustments to maintain equilibrium. Increased sway variability is one of the earliest predictors of balance decline. AI systems measure sway patterns across multiple axes, identifying directional biases and instability signatures that correlate with future fall risk. Unlike static clinical tests that capture a single moment, AI evaluates sway across environments, times of day, and fatigue states, building a comprehensive profile of balance integrity.

Artificial intelligence also excels at identifying asymmetry. The human body is not perfectly symmetrical, but increasing asymmetry over time is a strong predictor of instability. AI tracks how force is distributed between limbs, how joints move relative to one another, and how the center of mass shifts during motion. These insights reveal compensatory patterns that may stem from old injuries, joint degeneration, or neuromuscular inefficiencies. Early detection allows for targeted correction before asymmetry becomes entrenched and destabilizing.

Environmental context further enhances AI's predictive power. Balance is not tested in isolation; it is challenged by real-world conditions such as uneven surfaces, low lighting, multitasking, and cognitive load. AI systems incorporate contextual data to understand how balance responds under varying conditions. This enables the identification of scenario-specific risks, such as instability during turns, transitions, or distraction. Rather than issuing generalized warnings, AI provides situational awareness that empowers individuals to adjust behavior intelligently.

Another critical advantage of AI-based instability detection is its ability to learn the individual baseline. Traditional assessments compare people to population averages, which often obscures meaningful change. AI compares each person to their own historical data, detecting deviation rather than deficiency. This personalized approach ensures that early warnings are accurate and relevant, reducing false alarms while increasing sensitivity to genuine decline.

Importantly, AI does not merely detect risk; it contextualizes it. Instead of labeling someone as "high risk," AI systems identify which components of balance are changing and why. This transforms detection into actionable insight. Interventions become specific, efficient, and targeted, addressing root causes rather than symptoms. By detecting instability early, AI enables a shift from reactive care to proactive preservation.

This chapter reframes fall risk as a data-driven phenomenon rather than an unpredictable event. Artificial intelligence reveals that instability leaves a trail long before it results in injury. By learning to read that trail, individuals gain the opportunity to intervene while confidence, strength, and independence are still intact. Detection is not about fear—it is about foresight. AI provides that foresight with unprecedented clarity.

"The Step That Never Happened"

David had always trusted his body. At fifty-eight, he still considered himself agile, capable, and steady. He hiked regularly, worked in his garden, and prided himself on staying active. When his employer introduced an optional AI-powered wellness monitoring program, David signed up out of curiosity rather than concern. He expected reassurance. What he received instead was information.

The system began quietly, collecting data from his daily movements. Weeks passed without comment. Then one afternoon, a notification appeared—not an alarm, but a trend. The AI had detected increasing variability in David's left-side load transfer during turns, particularly late in the day. Reaction timing in his stabilizing muscles had slowed slightly, correlating with periods of mental fatigue. None of this matched how David felt. He felt fine. That disconnect unsettled him more than a warning would have.

At first, David dismissed the findings. But as he reviewed the visualizations, patterns emerged. The changes were subtle, gradual, and consistent. They didn't suggest imminent danger, only direction. The AI wasn't predicting a fall—it was mapping a trajectory. That distinction mattered. It felt informative rather than threatening.

With guidance, David began targeted adjustments. He modified his movement routines, incorporated specific activation drills, and adjusted his daily workload to account for fatigue-related instability. He didn't reduce activity; he refined it. Over time, the data stabilized. Variability decreased. Timing improved. Confidence followed naturally, without effort.

Months later, while stepping off a ladder during yard work, David felt his foot slip slightly. Instinctively, his body corrected. The moment passed unnoticed by anyone else. But David paused, heart racing—not from fear, but from awareness. He realized that the correction felt automatic, strong, and controlled. Later that day, he checked his movement data. Stability metrics had held steady under stress.

That was when it struck him: the fall that could have happened never did. Not because of luck, but because instability had been detected early and addressed intelligently. The AI hadn't wrapped him in caution. It had quietly reinforced his resilience.

David still trusted his body—but now he trusted the information supporting it. He moved with the same confidence as before, unaware most days of the system working in the background. And that was the point. The best prevention, he realized, is invisible. It doesn't announce itself. It simply ensures that the step that could have changed everything never happens.

Chapter 3

Retraining Balance, Coordination, and Confidence Using AI-Guided Intervention

Detecting instability is only the beginning. The true power of artificial intelligence in mobility preservation lies not just in identifying risk, but in guiding precise, adaptive retraining that restores balance, coordination, and physical confidence. Once instability patterns are identified, AI systems shift from observation to intervention, translating complex movement data into actionable strategies that recalibrate how the body stabilizes itself. This transformation marks a fundamental shift away from generic balance exercises toward intelligent, responsive retraining tailored to the individual's unique neuromuscular profile.

Balance retraining is most effective when it addresses timing rather than force. Traditional approaches often emphasize strength, yet strength alone does not restore stability if muscles activate out of sequence or too late to prevent loss of equilibrium. AI-guided systems prioritize neuromuscular timing, teaching the body to respond more efficiently to perturbations by refining activation patterns across stabilizing muscle groups. Through repeated, data-informed feedback loops, AI helps retrain the nervous system to anticipate instability and respond reflexively, restoring automatic balance responses that degrade with age.

Coordination is central to this process. As people age, movements become more segmented and cautious, reducing fluidity and adaptability. AI-guided retraining encourages variability rather than rigidity, reintroducing controlled challenges that rebuild the body's ability to adjust dynamically. By monitoring how the body adapts to these challenges, AI continuously refines intervention strategies, increasing difficulty only when stability improves. This ensures progress without overexposure to risk, a balance that is difficult to achieve through intuition alone.

One of the most transformative aspects of AI intervention is its personalization. Balance deficits rarely stem from a single cause. For some individuals, instability originates in delayed proprioceptive feedback. For others, it arises from joint stiffness, muscular inhibition, or cognitive-motor interference. AI systems identify which pathways are compromised and prioritize retraining accordingly. This targeted approach accelerates improvement while reducing unnecessary effort, making retraining sustainable rather than burdensome. Artificial intelligence also plays a crucial role in rebuilding confidence. Loss of balance confidence often persists even after physical capacity improves, leading to guarded movement patterns that increase fall risk. AI provides objective evidence of improvement through measurable metrics such as reduced sway variability, improved reaction timing, and restored symmetry. This data-driven reassurance helps recalibrate perception, allowing individuals to trust their bodies again. Confidence, once restored, reinforces physical gains by encouraging natural movement rather than avoidance.

Another advantage of AI-guided retraining is adaptability across environments. Balance is context-dependent, and improvements achieved in controlled settings may not transfer to real-world conditions. AI systems monitor movement across daily activities, adjusting interventions to ensure that gains generalize beyond isolated exercises. This integration of training with real-life movement accelerates functional recovery and enhances long-term resilience.

Fatigue and cognitive load are also accounted for in AI-guided retraining. Balance often deteriorates when individuals are tired, stressed, or distracted. AI systems identify these vulnerabilities and incorporate resilience training that strengthens stability under less-than-ideal conditions. This holistic approach ensures that balance improvements hold when they matter most, such as during multitasking or unfamiliar environments.

Ultimately, AI-guided intervention reframes balance retraining as a collaborative process between human adaptability and machine intelligence. The goal is not to impose rigid control but to restore the body's natural capacity for self-correction. By continuously learning from individual responses, AI systems refine retraining strategies over time, ensuring that improvements are maintained rather than lost. This chapter demonstrates that balance decline is not a one-way path. With intelligent guidance, coordination can be retrained, confidence can be restored, and mobility can remain a source of freedom rather than fear.

"Learning to Trust the Turn"

Elena noticed the problem while dancing in her kitchen. Music had always pulled movement out of her effortlessly, but lately she avoided turning too quickly. Spins felt uncertain. Even simple pivots made her pause. At fifty-six, she didn't think of herself as fragile, yet something in her body hesitated when rotation was involved. She adapted by moving slower, keeping her feet planted, telling herself it was just a preference. Deep down, she knew it was caution.

When Elena enrolled in an AI-guided mobility program recommended by her physical therapist, she expected strength exercises. Instead, the system focused on timing and coordination. Data from her movements revealed delayed stabilization during rotational transitions, particularly when shifting weight from one foot to the other. The AI didn't label her weak. It identified hesitation—a lag between intention and execution.

The retraining began gently. Subtle challenges encouraged fluid turns, monitored closely by the system. Feedback wasn't intrusive; it was informative. Over time, Elena learned to move through uncertainty rather than around it. The AI adjusted difficulty as her coordination improved, never pushing faster than her nervous system could adapt. Each successful turn rebuilt trust, not just in her body, but in her ability to respond.

Weeks passed. One evening, music played again in the kitchen. Without thinking, Elena turned. The movement was smooth, automatic, joyful. She stopped mid-laugh, surprised not by the turn itself, but by the absence of fear. Later, reviewing her progress metrics, she saw the evidence: improved reaction timing, reduced asymmetry, restored rotational stability.

Months later, Elena found herself navigating a crowded market, weaving effortlessly through movement and noise. She realized she no longer planned her steps. Confidence had returned quietly, reinforced by countless micro-successes guided by intelligent feedback. The AI hadn't taught her how to move. It had reminded her how to trust movement again.

Elena still danced. She still turned. And each turn reinforced the truth she had rediscovered: balance is not just physical. It is a conversation between trust and response. With the right guidance, that conversation can be restored.

Chapter 4

How AI Adapts Environments to Reinforce Stability in Real Life

Balance does not exist in isolation. It is continuously shaped by the environments in which the body moves. Flooring texture, lighting conditions, furniture layout, footwear transitions, stair geometry, and even habitual walking paths influence stability in subtle but powerful ways. As people age, the margin for error within these environments narrows, not because individuals become incapable, but because environmental demands increasingly exceed the body's adaptive capacity. Artificial intelligence transforms how environments are understood by shifting them from static backdrops into dynamic components of mobility preservation. Instead of forcing the body to compensate endlessly, AI helps environments adapt intelligently to support stability, confidence, and freedom of movement.

Traditional fall-prevention strategies often rely on generic recommendations such as removing rugs, installing handrails, or improving lighting. While helpful, these approaches treat all individuals the same and assume risk is evenly distributed across spaces. AI-driven environmental adaptation replaces assumption with measurement. By analyzing how an individual moves through specific spaces, AI identifies where instability emerges and why. A hallway may appear safe yet consistently produce gait variability due to lighting glare or visual contrast issues. A staircase may induce hesitation not because of strength deficits, but because step depth disrupts rhythm. AI uncovers these relationships by correlating movement data with environmental context.

One of the most valuable contributions of AI is its ability to detect transition-related instability. Most falls occur not during steady walking, but during transitions such as standing up, turning, stepping down, or navigating thresholds. These moments challenge coordination and sensory integration simultaneously. AI systems map where transitions occur in daily life and analyze how the body responds to them over time. This allows for targeted environmental modifications that reduce risk without limiting movement. Instead of advising avoidance, AI enables redesign.

Lighting is a prime example. Aging increases reliance on visual input for balance, yet poor lighting conditions can distort depth perception and delay corrective responses. AI systems identify patterns of instability correlated with low light, glare, or contrast shifts. Rather than recommending blanket brightness increases, AI supports precision lighting strategies that enhance depth cues and reduce visual noise. The result is improved stability without altering lifestyle or aesthetics.

Flooring surfaces also play a critical role. Subtle differences in friction, texture, or compliance can alter gait mechanics. AI systems detect changes in stride and load distribution across different surfaces, identifying those that increase instability. This insight allows individuals to make informed choices about flooring materials, footwear, or surface treatments that align with their movement profile. Importantly, AI does not seek to eliminate challenge entirely; it calibrates it, ensuring that environments remain engaging while safe.

Furniture layout and spatial flow further influence balance confidence. Narrow pathways, sharp turns, or poorly placed obstacles increase cognitive load and disrupt natural movement patterns. AI-driven analysis highlights areas where navigation becomes inefficient or destabilizing, enabling redesigns that enhance flow rather than restrict space. These adjustments preserve independence by making environments intuitive rather than cautious.

Artificial intelligence also adapts environments dynamically. Smart home systems integrated with AI mobility analysis adjust lighting, alerts, and spatial cues based on real-time conditions such as fatigue, time of day, or recent activity levels. This responsiveness ensures that environmental support scales with need, reinforcing stability without constant conscious effort.

Crucially, AI reframes environmental adaptation as empowerment rather than limitation. The goal is not to create sterile, overly protected spaces, but to support confident movement through thoughtful design. By aligning environments with human adaptability, AI reduces the cognitive and physical burden placed on aging bodies, allowing movement to remain fluid and self-directed.

This chapter underscores a fundamental principle: preserving mobility is not solely about changing the body. It is about harmonizing the relationship between the body and its surroundings. Artificial intelligence enables this harmony by revealing how environments shape stability moment by moment. When environments adapt intelligently, balance becomes less about vigilance and more about freedom. AI does not confine movement—it quietly supports it, ensuring that daily spaces remain allies rather than obstacles as we age.

"The House That Learned With Him"

Thomas had lived in the same home for over thirty years. Every corner was familiar. Every step had been taken thousands of times. That familiarity made the change harder to accept. At sixty-five, he began noticing moments of hesitation—nothing dramatic, just a pause before stepping into the shower, a slight lean when navigating the hallway at night, an unconscious reach for furniture while turning. The house hadn't changed, but his relationship with it had.

When Thomas's mobility data was analyzed through an AI-supported program, the insights surprised him. Instability wasn't constant; it appeared in specific places at specific times. The hallway at dusk. The transition from carpet to tile. The stair landing where light shifted abruptly. None of these areas felt dangerous, yet the data told a consistent story. His body was adapting quietly, compensating for environmental demands he had stopped noticing.

Instead of suggesting drastic changes, the AI guided small, precise adjustments. Lighting was refined to improve depth perception. Visual contrast was subtly enhanced at transitions. Furniture was repositioned to improve flow rather than provide support. Even footwear recommendations were tailored to how his gait responded to different surfaces. The house didn't become restrictive. It became responsive.

Over time, Thomas stopped thinking about where he placed his feet. Movement regained its ease. One evening, as he walked through the hallway without hesitation, he realized something had shifted. The house felt familiar again—not because nothing had changed, but because it had changed with him. Months later, a visiting friend remarked on how "comfortable" the home felt, unable to identify why. Thomas smiled, understanding something deeper. His environment was no longer something he navigated carefully. It supported him quietly, intelligently, without demanding attention.

Thomas hadn't lost independence. He had reinforced it. The house didn't protect him from movement; it encouraged it. And in that encouragement, confidence returned. The home had learned with him, adapting not to age, but to preserve freedom within it.

Chapter 5

How AI Optimizes Footwear, Assistive Tools, and Daily Equipment for Lifelong Stability

Mobility begins at the point of contact between the body and the ground. Feet, footwear, and the tools we use to interact with our environment form the foundation of balance, yet they are among the most underestimated contributors to instability as we age. Small mismatches between footwear design and an individual's movement mechanics can amplify imbalance, disrupt gait efficiency, and increase fall risk without obvious warning signs. Artificial intelligence introduces precision into this overlooked domain by transforming footwear and assistive tools from generic products into personalized mobility extensions that actively support balance rather than passively existing beneath it.

Traditional footwear recommendations often rely on broad categories such as "supportive," "cushioned," or "stable," which fail to account for individual differences in gait patterns, pressure distribution, joint alignment, and neuromuscular timing. AI-guided mobility systems analyze how forces travel through the foot during standing, walking, and turning, identifying where instability originates. For some individuals, excessive cushioning delays proprioceptive feedback, reducing the body's ability to respond quickly to changes in terrain. For others, insufficient shock absorption increases joint stiffness and compensatory movement. AI identifies these distinctions, allowing footwear selection to be optimized for balance rather than fashion or habit.

Footwear optimization is not about correction alone; it is about communication. The feet serve as sensory organs, relaying information about surface texture, slope, and movement dynamics to the nervous system. Aging dulls this feedback loop, increasing reliance on vision and conscious control. AI systems evaluate how different footwear designs influence sensory input and reaction timing, recommending options that restore efficient communication between the feet and brain. This subtle enhancement improves stability without requiring conscious effort, allowing movement to remain automatic and confident.

Assistive tools such as walking poles, canes, braces, and wearable supports are similarly transformed by AI. Historically, these tools were introduced reactively, often signaling perceived decline and discouraging use due to stigma or discomfort. AI reframes assistive technology as performance-enhancing rather than compensatory. By analyzing when and where instability occurs, AI determines whether a tool is needed continuously, intermittently, or not at all. This precision prevents overreliance while providing targeted support when risk is highest, such as during fatigue, unfamiliar environments, or complex transitions.

Artificial intelligence also guides proper tool selection and usage. An improperly sized or incorrectly used assistive device can increase instability rather than reduce it. AI systems assess how tools interact with movement patterns, ensuring alignment with individual biomechanics. This dynamic feedback ensures that assistive tools enhance balance rather than interfere with natural movement, preserving autonomy while reducing risk.

Beyond footwear and traditional assistive devices, AI extends into everyday equipment such as backpacks, handbags, grocery carts, and even mobile devices. Load distribution, hand occupancy, and posture all influence balance. AI identifies how these factors affect stability, offering recommendations that minimize disruption without limiting daily activities. This holistic approach acknowledges that balance is influenced by how we carry our lives, not just how we walk.

Importantly, AI-driven optimization adapts over time. As strength, coordination, and confidence improve, recommendations evolve. Tools may be phased out, modified, or repurposed. Conversely, as new challenges emerge, AI reintroduces support proactively. This adaptability ensures that mobility aids remain aligned with actual needs rather than outdated assumptions.

This chapter emphasizes a critical insight: preserving balance is not solely about training the body, but about equipping it intelligently. Footwear and tools are not signs of weakness; they are interfaces between human adaptability and environmental demands. Artificial intelligence elevates these interfaces from static objects to dynamic partners in mobility preservation. When chosen and used with precision, they extend independence, reinforce confidence, and support lifelong movement without diminishing identity or autonomy.

"The Shoes He Never Thought About"

Carlos had worn the same style of shoes for decades. Comfortable, familiar, reliable. When he began noticing occasional instability during long walks, he blamed fatigue and shrugged it off. At sixty, he wasn't ready to reconsider something as personal as footwear. Shoes were just shoes. Or so he thought.

After enrolling in an AI-guided mobility program following a minor stumble, Carlos agreed to a full movement analysis. The data revealed something unexpected. His shoes, while comfortable, were delaying sensory feedback and increasing lateral instability during turns. The cushioning he loved was muting information his nervous system needed. It wasn't dramatic. It was cumulative.

Reluctantly, Carlos tried AI-recommended alternatives tailored to his gait mechanics. The difference was subtle at first—slightly more awareness of the ground, slightly quicker response when changing direction. Over time, the change became unmistakable. Walks felt smoother. Turns felt natural again. The hesitation he had accepted as normal began to fade.

The AI system also recommended a lightweight walking pole for longer hikes, not as a crutch, but as a performance enhancer during fatigue. Carlos resisted initially, worried about appearances. But the data showed improved symmetry and reduced strain. He tried it once. Then again. Soon, it became part of his routine—not because he needed it, but because it made movement feel effortless.

Months later, Carlos found himself navigating a busy airport, carrying luggage and moving with ease. He realized he hadn't thought about balance once. The tools worked quietly, supporting him without demanding attention. His identity hadn't changed. His confidence had grown.

Carlos still wore shoes every day. But now, he wore the right ones. And in that choice, mobility stopped being something he managed and became something he enjoyed again. The support was invisible. The freedom was not.

Chapter 6

How AI Manages Fatigue, Multitasking, and Cognitive Load to Preserve Balance

Balance is not purely physical. It is deeply cognitive. The brain must continuously allocate attention, process sensory input, and coordinate motor responses, all while managing competing demands such as conversation, decision-making, emotional regulation, and environmental awareness. As people age, this cognitive load becomes a critical factor in instability, often surpassing strength or coordination as the primary contributor to falls. Artificial intelligence reveals that many balance failures do not occur because the body is incapable, but because the brain is overloaded. Understanding and managing this load is essential for preserving mobility, and AI provides unprecedented tools to do so intelligently.

Cognitive-motor interference occurs when the brain is required to perform more than one task simultaneously, such as walking while talking, navigating crowds, or carrying objects while making decisions. In younger individuals, these tasks are seamlessly integrated. With age, however, neural efficiency declines subtly, reducing the brain's ability to manage parallel processing. This results in delayed reactions, compromised balance responses, and increased instability during everyday activities. AI systems identify when and how cognitive load impacts movement by correlating balance metrics with mental engagement levels, revealing patterns that traditional assessments overlook.

Fatigue amplifies these effects. Physical fatigue reduces muscle responsiveness, while mental fatigue slows decision-making and reaction time. Together, they create a compounding effect that dramatically increases fall risk. AI-driven mobility systems monitor indicators of fatigue through changes in gait variability, reaction timing, postural sway, and movement efficiency. These systems do not merely detect fatigue; they contextualize it, identifying when fatigue becomes destabilizing rather than simply uncomfortable.

One of the most powerful capabilities of AI is its ability to differentiate between productive challenge and destabilizing overload. Not all cognitive load is harmful. Controlled multitasking can strengthen neural resilience and improve balance adaptability. AI-guided systems introduce cognitive challenges incrementally, monitoring how the body responds and adjusting difficulty in real time. This ensures that individuals build cognitive-motor resilience without crossing thresholds that increase risk. Artificial intelligence also enables strategic pacing. By learning individual fatigue patterns, AI systems recommend activity timing, rest intervals, and task sequencing that preserve stability throughout the day. Instead of advising blanket rest or reduced activity, AI optimizes engagement, allowing individuals to remain active while minimizing risk. This proactive approach prevents the spiral of avoidance that often follows fatigue-related instability.

Environmental and situational awareness further enhance AI's effectiveness. Balance challenges differ in familiar versus unfamiliar environments, quiet versus crowded spaces, and predictable versus unpredictable settings. AI systems integrate contextual data to identify high-risk scenarios, enabling preemptive strategies such as slowing pace, simplifying tasks, or increasing environmental support. This situational intelligence transforms balance management from reactive caution into informed decision-making.

Crucially, AI reframes multitasking not as a threat but as a trainable skill. By identifying specific cognitive loads that disrupt balance, AI enables targeted retraining that improves dual-task performance. This restores the ability to move confidently while thinking, conversing, and engaging with the world—an essential component of independence and quality of life.

This chapter highlights a vital truth: balance preservation requires managing the brain as much as the body. Artificial intelligence illuminates the invisible role of cognition in stability, offering tools to monitor, train, and protect balance under real-world conditions. By addressing fatigue and cognitive load intelligently, AI ensures that mobility remains resilient not just in ideal circumstances, but in the complex, multitasking reality of everyday life.

"The Conversation That Changed Her Pace"

Linda had always been a multitasker. At fifty-nine, she prided herself on efficiency—walking while checking her phone, talking while navigating busy sidewalks, carrying groceries while planning dinner. When she stumbled one afternoon while chatting with a neighbor, she laughed it off. But the incident lingered in her mind. It wasn't the stumble that worried her. It was the surprise.

When Linda's movement data was later analyzed through an AI-supported mobility program, the findings were clear. Her balance metrics remained strong during focused walking, but degraded significantly during conversation and decision-making tasks. The AI didn't suggest weakness. It identified overload. Her brain was juggling more than her balance system could reliably support under certain conditions.

Instead of restricting activity, the AI guided awareness. Linda learned to recognize when cognitive load peaked—late afternoons, crowded environments, emotionally engaging conversations. The system suggested subtle pacing adjustments, brief pauses, and strategic task sequencing. These changes didn't limit her life; they refined it.

Over time, Linda engaged in AI-guided dual-task training designed to strengthen cognitive-motor integration. Simple challenges gradually increased complexity, always monitored for stability. Confidence grew alongside capability. Walking while talking no longer felt risky. It felt practiced.

One day, Linda found herself navigating a busy market, holding a conversation while weaving through crowds. Halfway through, she realized she hadn't once thought about balance. Her pace was natural. Her attention was flexible. The moment passed unnoticed—exactly as it should.

Later that evening, reviewing her progress, Linda understood what had changed. She hadn't slowed down her life. She had learned when to shift pace intelligently. The AI hadn't told her to stop multitasking. It had taught her how to do it safely.

Linda still talks, thinks, plans, and moves all at once. But now, she does so with awareness rather than assumption. The conversation that once caused hesitation had taught her something powerful: balance is not about doing less. It's about knowing when—and how—to do more.

Chapter 7

How AI Forecasts Mobility Decline and Protects Independence Over Time

Preserving mobility is not a short-term goal. It is a long-term strategy that unfolds across decades, shaped by thousands of small decisions, adaptations, and environmental interactions. While traditional approaches to aging focus on reacting to decline after it appears, artificial intelligence introduces a fundamentally different model: forecasting. By identifying patterns that precede mobility loss, AI allows individuals to intervene years before instability becomes limiting. This shift—from response to anticipation—represents one of the most powerful applications of AI in aging and independence preservation.

Mobility decline follows recognizable trajectories. Changes in gait variability, reaction timing, asymmetry, fatigue tolerance, and cognitive-motor integration rarely occur randomly. They evolve in predictable sequences influenced by genetics, lifestyle, environment, and health history. AI systems trained on large-scale longitudinal data recognize these trajectories and compare them against individual movement profiles. This enables forecasting not in terms of inevitable outcomes, but in terms of probability and timing. Instead of asking whether decline will occur, AI asks when, how, and under what conditions it is most likely to emerge.

Forecasting allows mobility to be managed proactively rather than defensively. AI models identify early inflection points—moments when small adjustments produce disproportionate benefits. These moments often occur long before noticeable impairment, when adaptability remains high and interventions are most effective. By surfacing these windows of opportunity, AI empowers individuals to act early, preserving function with far less effort than would be required later.

One of the most important insights AI provides is the distinction between chronological age and functional age. Two individuals of the same age may have vastly different mobility trajectories based on movement patterns, resilience, and adaptability. AI evaluates functional age dynamically, allowing goals and strategies to be aligned with actual capacity rather than assumptions. This personalized forecasting prevents both overconfidence and unnecessary restriction, supporting realistic, empowering planning.

Artificial intelligence also integrates mobility forecasting with broader life planning. Travel, work, caregiving, housing, and lifestyle choices all place different demands on balance and movement. AI helps individuals anticipate how future plans intersect with mobility trends, allowing for informed decisions that preserve independence. This may involve targeted retraining before increased activity, environmental adaptation before relocation, or pacing strategies during demanding life phases. Forecasting transforms mobility from a constraint into a design variable.

Importantly, AI forecasting is not static. It evolves continuously as new data is collected, reflecting real changes rather than projections frozen in time. Improvements in balance, coordination, and resilience update forecasts, reinforcing positive behaviors and revealing the long-term impact of interventions. Conversely, emerging risks prompt timely adjustments. This dynamic feedback loop ensures that mobility planning remains responsive rather than prescriptive.

Psychologically, forecasting reduces anxiety by replacing uncertainty with clarity. Fear of the unknown often drives overcautious behavior that accelerates decline. AI provides evidence-based reassurance, showing not only where risks exist, but where stability is strong. This balanced perspective supports confidence grounded in data rather than denial or fear.

This chapter completes the framework introduced throughout the book. Detection identifies early signals. Retraining restores function. Environmental adaptation reinforces stability. Tools and cognitive strategies support daily life. Forecasting unifies these elements into a coherent, forward-looking system that protects independence over time. Artificial intelligence does not promise agelessness. It offers something far more valuable: foresight. With foresight, mobility becomes manageable, adaptable, and resilient across the lifespan.

"Planning the Long Walk"

Robert had always been a planner. At sixty-three, he was mapping the next chapter of his life—travel, volunteering, long walks in unfamiliar cities. What unsettled him wasn't aging itself, but uncertainty. He felt capable now, but wondered how long that would last. Rather than waiting for answers to arrive uninvited, he enrolled in an AI-guided mobility forecasting program.

The system didn't predict decline. It mapped possibilities. Based on Robert's movement patterns, fatigue responses, and balance metrics, the AI outlined potential trajectories—some stable, some vulnerable under specific conditions. Long days of walking without recovery. Crowded environments late in the evening. Uneven terrain when cognitively distracted. None of this surprised Robert. What surprised him was how actionable it felt. Instead of limiting plans, Robert adjusted preparation. He engaged in targeted retraining months before travel. He adapted footwear and pacing strategies. He learned when to rest—not out of weakness, but strategy. As his data improved, forecasts shifted. Risk windows narrowed. Confidence grew.

On a trip abroad, Robert walked miles each day, navigating cobblestones and crowds. One evening, he paused at the edge of a plaza, watching people move effortlessly through space. He realized he was doing the same. Not because he ignored risk, but because he had planned for it.

Back home, reviewing his updated mobility forecast, Robert saw stability extending further into the future than when he had begun. The AI hadn't promised certainty. It had given him something better: direction. He wasn't walking blindly into the years ahead. He was walking informed.

The long walk he had planned wasn't just across cities. It was across time. And with foresight, preparation, and intelligent support, Robert understood that independence wasn't something you lose suddenly. It's something you protect—step by step—when you know where you're going.

Chapter 8

How AI Creates Continuous Protection Through Health Systems, Alerts, and Support Networks

Mobility does not exist in isolation from healthcare, family, or community systems. As people age, balance and movement become increasingly influenced by medications, acute illnesses, stressors, and environmental disruptions that lie outside daily routines. Even individuals with strong balance systems can experience sudden vulnerability during moments of illness, dehydration, sleep disruption, or emotional shock. Artificial intelligence extends mobility protection beyond self-management by integrating balance intelligence into broader health, alert, and support networks that provide continuous protection without constant vigilance.

Traditional healthcare models assess mobility episodically, often during annual visits or after an incident has occurred. This leaves long gaps during which subtle decline, acute risk, or temporary instability can go unnoticed. AI bridges this gap by continuously monitoring movement patterns and contextualizing them within health data, medication changes, sleep quality, hydration, and stress markers. When instability emerges suddenly rather than gradually, AI distinguishes between chronic decline and acute disruption, enabling timely response rather than delayed intervention.

One of the most powerful applications of AI in mobility protection is early warning. Sudden increases in sway, delayed reaction timing, or altered gait patterns may signal underlying issues such as infection, medication side effects, cardiovascular stress, or neurological disruption. AI systems detect these deviations from baseline rapidly and flag them for attention, often before symptoms become obvious. This transforms balance monitoring into a form of early health surveillance that protects both mobility and overall well-being.

AI-enabled alert systems are designed not to alarm unnecessarily, but to escalate intelligently. Low-level alerts may prompt rest, hydration, or environmental adjustment. Higher-risk patterns trigger notifications to caregivers, clinicians, or family members, depending on predefined preferences. This graduated response model preserves autonomy while ensuring support is available when needed. Importantly, AI does not replace human judgment; it augments it by ensuring that critical information is delivered at the right moment.

Integration with healthcare providers further enhances this protective network. AI-generated mobility reports provide clinicians with objective, longitudinal data that improves diagnostic accuracy and treatment decisions. Rather than relying on patient recall or single-moment assessments, providers gain insight into how mobility changes over time and under different conditions. This supports more precise medication management, rehabilitation planning, and preventive care.

Support networks also benefit from AI-guided insight. Family members often struggle to distinguish between normal aging and emerging risk, leading either to excessive worry or delayed concern. AI provides clarity by translating movement data into understandable trends and thresholds. This shared understanding fosters proactive support without undermining independence, strengthening trust rather than tension within relationships.

Artificial intelligence also plays a critical role during recovery periods. After illness, injury, or hospitalization, mobility often declines temporarily. AI systems monitor recovery trajectories, ensuring that stability returns to baseline rather than plateauing at a lower level. This prevents temporary setbacks from becoming permanent losses, reinforcing long-term independence. At its core, AI-enabled protection reframes safety as a continuous process rather than an emergency response. It acknowledges that vulnerability is situational, not permanent, and that support should scale with need rather than replace autonomy. By embedding mobility intelligence into health and support systems, AI creates a safety net that is always present but rarely intrusive.

This chapter completes the transformation of mobility from a personal responsibility into a shared, intelligent ecosystem. Artificial intelligence does not watch over individuals to control them. It stands quietly behind them, ready to inform, alert, and support when conditions shift. In doing so, it preserves what matters most—not just safety, but dignity, confidence, and the freedom to live fully without fear of sudden loss.

"The Alert That Came Early"

Janet never considered herself at risk. At sixty-seven, she lived alone, stayed active, and valued her independence fiercely. When her doctor suggested integrating AI-based mobility monitoring into her health plan, she agreed only because it promised to stay out of her way. She wanted reassurance, not supervision.

For months, nothing happened. Her movement data remained stable. The system stayed silent. Then one morning, Janet felt unusually tired. She moved more slowly, assuming she hadn't slept well. What she didn't feel was instability. What she didn't know was that her gait symmetry had changed, her reaction timing had slowed, and her postural sway had increased beyond her normal range.

The AI system noticed immediately. It didn't trigger an emergency. It issued a gentle alert suggesting rest and hydration. When the pattern persisted, it escalated quietly, notifying her healthcare provider with a concise summary of the deviation. A follow-up call led to testing that revealed an early infection—caught days before serious symptoms would have appeared.

Janet recovered quickly. More importantly, her mobility returned fully to baseline. Reviewing her data afterward, she realized something profound. She hadn't fallen. She hadn't been frightened. She hadn't lost control. The system had intervened early enough that nothing dramatic needed to happen.

Weeks later, Janet updated her preferences to include her daughter as a secondary contact—not because she felt weaker, but because she felt supported. The system wasn't watching her. It was standing behind her.

Janet still lives alone. She still moves freely. But now, when she steps outside each morning, she does so knowing that if something changes—suddenly, silently, unexpectedly—she won't face it alone. The protection is invisible. The confidence is not.

Chapter 9

Trust, Privacy, and Ethical Use of AI in Mobility Monitoring

As artificial intelligence becomes increasingly embedded in mobility preservation, an essential question emerges: how do we protect independence without compromising privacy? The same systems capable of detecting instability, forecasting decline, and alerting support networks rely on continuous data collection. Movement patterns, health indicators, environmental interactions, and behavioral rhythms are analyzed to generate insight. While this intelligence offers profound benefits, it also introduces ethical responsibilities. Mobility protection must never come at the expense of autonomy, dignity, or personal control. Trust is not optional in AI systems that operate so intimately within daily life—it is foundational.

Trust begins with transparency. Individuals must understand what data is being collected, how it is processed, who can access it, and how long it is retained. Artificial intelligence systems designed for mobility support should prioritize clarity over complexity, presenting information in accessible language rather than technical abstraction. When users comprehend how the system functions, fear decreases and engagement increases. Opacity breeds suspicion; transparency builds partnership.

Privacy in AI mobility systems is not merely about data security; it is about contextual integrity. Movement data may reveal patterns of daily life, routines, and vulnerabilities. Ethical systems minimize unnecessary data collection and prioritize anonymization where possible. Advanced encryption and decentralized processing ensure that sensitive information is protected not only from external threats but from misuse within organizations. AI must serve individuals—not exploit them.

Consent is another critical pillar. Ethical AI systems allow users to define boundaries regarding data sharing and alert thresholds. Some may choose to involve family members immediately during instability events, while others may prefer clinician-only notifications. Autonomy includes the right to calibrate support. AI mobility systems should empower individuals to adjust preferences easily, reinforcing the principle that assistance is configurable rather than imposed.

Another ethical dimension involves dependency. While AI offers guidance and protection, it must not erode personal agency. Systems should be designed to enhance self-awareness and decision-making rather than replace them. When individuals rely blindly on technology, resilience weakens. Ethical AI fosters education, providing explanations alongside recommendations, encouraging understanding rather than passive compliance.

Bias in AI systems must also be addressed. Algorithms trained on limited or non-diverse datasets risk misinterpreting movement patterns across different body types, cultural behaviors, or health conditions. Ethical design requires inclusive data modeling and continuous evaluation to prevent disparities in risk assessment. Mobility preservation must be equitable, not optimized for a narrow population subset.

There is also the psychological dimension of monitoring. Some individuals may initially perceive continuous data collection as surveillance. Ethical AI systems counter this perception by emphasizing collaboration rather than control. The narrative shifts from being watched to being supported. Language, interface design, and communication tone all influence this perception. Respectful design preserves dignity.

Importantly, ethical AI planning includes sunset protocols—clear guidelines for what happens when systems are discontinued, updated, or transferred. Data portability, deletion rights, and continuity safeguards ensure that individuals retain ownership of their mobility history. AI should never trap users within proprietary ecosystems without recourse.

Ultimately, trust in AI mobility systems is built not through promises, but through consistent, respectful performance. When alerts are accurate, data is secure, recommendations are transparent, and autonomy is preserved, confidence grows organically. Ethical AI does not demand trust; it earns it.

This chapter underscores a fundamental truth: technology that protects independence must itself operate within boundaries that respect independence. Artificial intelligence is a powerful ally in mobility preservation, but its legitimacy rests on integrity. When ethics guide innovation, AI becomes not a watcher, but a partner—supporting freedom without compromising privacy.

"The Choice to Share"

Evelyn valued her independence fiercely. At seventy, she lived alone by choice, proud of her ability to manage her home, her schedule, and her health without interference. When her physician suggested integrating AI mobility monitoring after a minor imbalance incident, she hesitated—not because she doubted the technology, but because she feared losing control.

The system was explained carefully. Evelyn would own her data. She could decide who received alerts. She could disable sharing at any time. The AI would analyze movement locally before transmitting only essential summaries. Nothing would be visible without her consent. The decision remained hers.

For weeks, Evelyn kept notifications private. She reviewed her stability metrics quietly, adjusting routines without involving anyone else. Then one afternoon, after a medication adjustment, her balance metrics shifted abruptly. The system flagged increased sway and delayed reaction timing. Evelyn felt slightly off but not alarmed. The AI suggested contacting her physician. She did.

The medication dosage was corrected early, preventing a potential fall. Reviewing the event, Evelyn realized something important: the system had not acted without her. It had informed her. The decision to share data with her daughter afterward was not driven by fear, but by clarity. She expanded her alert settings voluntarily, defining exactly when and how notifications would be sent.

Months later, when a brief episode of dizziness occurred during a heatwave, her daughter received a calm, contextual alert rather than an emergency panic. They spoke briefly, adjusted hydration and rest, and the moment passed. No ambulance. No drama. Just informed action. Evelyn reflected on her initial hesitation. She had feared surveillance. What she experienced instead was partnership. The system did not intrude. It supported. It did not override her choices. It enhanced them.

Evelyn still controls her data. She reviews her metrics weekly, sometimes with curiosity, sometimes with reassurance. She understands what is monitored and why. Trust did not arrive instantly. It developed through transparency, consistency, and respect.

The choice to share was hers. And in making that choice consciously, she realized that independence is not about refusing support. It is about defining it.

Chapter 10

The Lifetime Mobility Blueprint: Designing Decades of Strength, Stability, and Independence

Mobility is not preserved by accident. It is preserved by design. The earlier chapters in this book have explored detection, retraining, environment, tools, cognitive resilience, forecasting, and ethical integration. Each element contributes to stability in the present moment. But long-term independence requires synthesis. Artificial intelligence enables not just reaction, not just correction, but orchestration—a coordinated system that aligns daily behavior, environmental structure, health management, and predictive modeling into a coherent blueprint for lifelong mobility.

The concept of a mobility blueprint reframes aging from a passive experience into an engineered trajectory. Instead of asking how to avoid decline, the question becomes how to shape adaptation. Every body changes over time. Muscle mass shifts, reaction time adjusts, sensory systems recalibrate. The objective is not to halt change but to guide it intelligently. AI-driven mobility systems allow individuals to observe how they are changing in real time, enabling them to adapt ahead of stress rather than after injury.

The lifetime blueprint begins with baseline clarity. Artificial intelligence establishes a comprehensive mobility profile—capturing gait variability, balance symmetry, reaction timing, fatigue thresholds, cognitive-motor resilience, environmental interaction patterns, and recovery rates. This baseline is not static; it evolves, but it provides orientation. Without orientation, planning becomes guesswork. With it, mobility becomes measurable.

Once baseline clarity is established, the blueprint incorporates structured adaptation cycles. Periods of challenge are followed by reinforcement. New environments are preceded by preparation. Increased activity levels are supported by targeted retraining. AI systems track how these cycles influence long-term metrics, identifying which strategies produce sustainable gains. Over years, this creates compounding stability—small improvements that reinforce one another rather than isolated interventions that fade.

The blueprint also integrates seasonal and life-phase transitions. Travel, relocation, retirement, caregiving responsibilities, illness, or new physical goals all alter mobility demands. AI forecasting anticipates how these shifts will intersect with individual movement patterns, recommending proactive modifications. Instead of being destabilized by change, individuals approach new phases equipped.

A key component of the lifetime blueprint is resilience reserve. Just as financial planning emphasizes emergency funds, mobility planning emphasizes adaptive reserve—the capacity to recover quickly from disruption. AI systems measure recovery speed following fatigue, illness, or environmental stress. Interventions are designed not only to maintain stability but to shorten recovery windows. This reserve protects independence during unexpected events.

Importantly, the blueprint evolves alongside identity. Mobility is deeply tied to self-perception. When individuals see themselves as capable, they move accordingly. AI reinforces this identity by providing objective evidence of strength and resilience. Confidence is no longer blind optimism; it is data-supported awareness. This alignment between perception and reality sustains engagement.

Another dimension of the lifetime blueprint is legacy planning. Mobility affects not only daily function but participation in family life, community contribution, and personal fulfillment. AI-guided systems ensure that physical capability aligns with long-term goals—whether that involves travel, volunteer work, physical hobbies, or multigenerational caregiving.

Independence is not defined by isolation but by active participation.

Artificial intelligence also ensures continuity. Data accumulated over years creates a longitudinal map of movement health. When healthcare providers engage, they access insight into decades of adaptation rather than snapshots. When life transitions occur, historical patterns inform decisions. This continuity transforms mobility from episodic management into lifelong stewardship.

Ultimately, the lifetime mobility blueprint represents a philosophical shift. Aging is no longer something that happens to the body. It becomes something the body navigates with informed guidance. AI does not replace discipline or awareness. It amplifies them. It ensures that the effort invested today compounds into stability tomorrow.

This final chapter affirms a central message: independence is not fragile when it is engineered. With continuous monitoring, adaptive retraining, environmental alignment, cognitive resilience, ethical integration, and long-term forecasting working together, mobility becomes durable. Artificial intelligence is not the star of the blueprint—it is the architect's tool. The individual remains the builder.

And when the builder plans decades ahead, movement

remains not just possible, but powerful.

"The Map Across the Years"

Michael turned seventy with a quiet determination. He did not fear aging, but he refused to drift through it unprepared. After experiencing minor instability following a bout of illness two years earlier, he had integrated AI mobility monitoring into his routine. What began as precaution became something deeper—a partnership that helped him see his future not as uncertainty, but as terrain.

Each year, Michael reviewed his mobility profile. He watched reaction times, symmetry scores, fatigue recovery curves. Some metrics improved with focused training. Others plateaued before rising again. The data did not judge him. It informed him. When travel was planned, he adjusted preparation months in advance. When winter reduced activity levels, he compensated deliberately.

At seventy-three, Michael experienced a brief hospitalization following a respiratory infection. In previous decades, such events often triggered long-term decline. But his mobility blueprint included recovery protocols. AI systems tracked his stability daily, guiding gradual reconditioning. Within weeks, his metrics returned to baseline. What could have marked a turning point became a temporary dip on a longer upward trend.

Years passed. At seventy-eight, Michael hiked moderate trails with his grandchildren. He did not move as quickly as he once had, but he moved confidently. The blueprint had adapted as he had. Environmental modifications in his home were subtle but intentional. Footwear evolved. Cognitive training remained integrated. Support networks were configured, though rarely needed.

On his eightieth birthday, Michael walked through a park at sunrise, reflecting on the decade behind him. He remembered the early hesitation after illness. He remembered choosing not to ignore it. He had not prevented aging. He had prepared for it.

Later that week, reviewing his longitudinal mobility data, he saw something that surprised him. Stability metrics had fluctuated but trended consistently upward in resilience. Recovery times shortened. Variability narrowed. The blueprint had worked—not because it eliminated risk, but because it transformed response.

Michael understood something simple and profound: independence is not the absence of vulnerability. It is the presence of preparation. The map he followed did not promise certainty. It offered direction.

As he stepped forward into his ninth decade, he did so not cautiously, but deliberately. Each step was informed by years of attention, adaptation, and intelligent support. The map across the years had not confined him. It had guided him.

And that guidance made all the difference.

Epilogue

The Future of Movement Is Designed, Not Left to Chance

Aging has long been framed as a gradual surrender. Strength fades. Reaction time slows. Balance becomes uncertain. Independence narrows. For generations, mobility decline was treated as a natural inevitability—managed only after it interfered with life. What this book has demonstrated is something fundamentally different. Mobility is not a passive outcome of time. It is an adaptive system influenced by awareness, environment, cognition, resilience, and design. And artificial intelligence has given us, for the first time in history, the ability to guide that adaptation deliberately.

The most powerful idea in this book is not that AI can prevent falls. It is that AI can prevent trajectories. Falls are visible events. Trajectories are invisible shifts unfolding months and years before those events occur. By detecting micro-changes in gait variability, reaction timing, asymmetry, fatigue tolerance, cognitive load response, and environmental interaction, AI transforms uncertainty into visibility. And visibility changes behavior.

When decline becomes visible early, intervention becomes smaller, easier, and more sustainable. When environmental instability is identified precisely, redesign becomes subtle rather than drastic. When fatigue patterns are mapped, pacing becomes intelligent rather than restrictive. When cognitive load thresholds are known, multitasking becomes strategic rather than risky. And when long-term forecasting reveals likely stress points years ahead, preparation replaces fear.

This is the true promise of AI mobility systems: not control, not surveillance, not technological dominance—but informed agency. Informed agency allows individuals to remain authors of their aging process. It shifts the narrative from "hoping to stay stable" to "engineering resilience."

Throughout this book, we explored how detection precedes correction, how retraining restores coordination, how environments adapt alongside the body, how tools enhance rather than signal decline, how fatigue and cognition influence stability, how forecasting protects decades, and how ethical design preserves dignity. These are not isolated innovations. They are components of a coherent ecosystem. When integrated, they create a mobility blueprint capable of extending independence far beyond what was once assumed possible.

But technology alone does not guarantee outcomes. AI is a tool. Its power depends on engagement. The individuals who benefit most are not those who monitor obsessively or rely blindly, but those who collaborate. They observe patterns, make adjustments, reassess, and refine. They treat mobility not as something to be defended in panic, but as something to be strengthened continuously.

It is also important to recognize that mobility preservation is not about perfection. There will be fluctuations. Illness will occur. Fatigue will appear. Recovery will take effort. AI does not eliminate vulnerability; it reduces unnecessary vulnerability. It shortens recovery windows. It provides early warning. It guides adaptation. And over time, these incremental advantages compound.

The future of aging will not be defined by medical breakthroughs alone. It will be shaped by intelligent systems that integrate movement, health, environment, and cognition into daily life. Mobility will become a monitored, optimized, and protected resource—like cardiovascular health or financial stability. Those who adopt these systems early will carry forward a quiet advantage: they will not age reactively. They will age strategically.

Ultimately, independence is not measured by the absence of assistance. It is measured by the presence of informed choice. Artificial intelligence, when ethically designed and consciously integrated, expands choice. It allows individuals to remain confident in unfamiliar environments, resilient during disruption, and prepared for transitions that once caused instability.

The question is no longer whether aging brings change. It is whether that change will be anticipated or endured. With intelligent mobility systems, it can be anticipated.

The future of movement is not accidental. It is designed. And those who design it step into the next decade not cautiously, but deliberately.

"The Last Thing She Feared"

When Eleanor turned eighty-five, her family expected her to slow down. They watched her carefully at gatherings, instinctively ready to steady her arm. Eleanor noticed. She appreciated the concern, but it did not match how she felt inside. She did not feel fragile. She felt prepared.

Fifteen years earlier, at seventy, she had experienced a minor fall in her garden. Nothing broke. Nothing dramatic happened. But it unsettled her. Instead of dismissing it, she chose to understand it. That choice led her into the world of AI-guided mobility monitoring. At first, she viewed it as an experiment. Over time, it became a partnership.

Eleanor tracked her movement metrics quietly. She learned her fatigue thresholds. She adjusted lighting in her home based on subtle instability patterns. She replaced rugs not because someone told her to, but because her data showed micro-variability at specific transitions. She trained cognitive-motor resilience deliberately. She adapted footwear precisely. She configured alert preferences thoughtfully, sharing only what she chose.

When illness struck at seventy-eight, the system detected instability early. Recovery protocols were initiated immediately. She regained baseline stability in weeks rather than months. When she moved homes at eighty-two, she pre-adapted her environment before unpacking boxes. She never experienced the "adjustment period" so common among peers.

At eighty-five, she walked daily in her neighborhood. Not quickly. Not recklessly. But confidently. One afternoon, as she navigated an uneven patch of sidewalk, her foot caught briefly on a crack. Her body corrected automatically. She paused, heart steady, surprised not by the stumble—but by the absence of fear.

That evening, reviewing her long-term mobility data, she saw a timeline stretching back fifteen years. There were dips and recoveries, fluctuations and reinforcements. But the trend was clear: resilience had strengthened. Recovery time had shortened. Instability windows had narrowed. Her granddaughter once asked her what she feared most about aging. Eleanor considered the question carefully. She did not fear falling. She did not fear slowing down. She did not even fear illness. What she had once feared was uncertainty.

And that was the one thing she no longer felt.

The system she chose years ago had not made her invincible. It had made her aware. And awareness, applied consistently over time, had preserved something far more valuable than speed or strength.

It had preserved her trust in her own steps.

On her eighty-fifth birthday, as her family gathered, Eleanor moved through the room naturally, accepting hugs without bracing, turning without hesitation, standing without assistance. They still watched her with care. But she did not feel watched.

She felt steady.

The last thing she feared was falling.

Because for fifteen years, she had not left her mobility to chance.

She had designed it.

www.ingramcontent.com/pod-product-compliance
Lightning Source LLC
LaVergne TN
LVHW022023200926
848481LV00007B/2504